IT'S TIME TO EAT PUMPKIN PIE

It's Time to Eat PUMPKIN PIE

Walter the Educator

Silent King Books
A WhichHead Entertainment Imprint

Copyright © 2024 by Walter the Educator

All rights reserved. No part of this book may be reproduced in any manner whatsoever without written per- mission except in the case of brief quotations embodied in critical articles and reviews.

First Printing, 2024

Disclaimer

This book is a literary work; the story is not about specific persons, locations, situations, and/or circumstances unless mentioned in a historical context. Any resemblance to real persons, locations, situations, and/or circumstances is coincidental. This book is for entertainment and informational purposes only. The author and publisher offer this information without warranties expressed or implied. No matter the grounds, neither the author nor the publisher will be accountable for any losses, injuries, or other damages caused by the reader's use of this book. The use of this book acknowledges an understanding and acceptance of this disclaimer.

It's Time to Eat PUMPKIN PIE is a collectible early learning book by Walter the Educator suitable for all ages belonging to Walter the Educator's Time to Eat Book Series. Collect more books at WaltertheEducator.com

USE THE EXTRA SPACE TO TAKE NOTES AND DOCUMENT YOUR MEMORIES

PUMPKIN PIE

The table is set, the smell's in the air,

It's Time to Eat

Pumpkin Pie

Pumpkin Pie is waiting there!

With a crust so flaky and spices so sweet,

It's finally time for a pumpkin treat.

Cinnamon, nutmeg, and sugar delight,

A pie so golden, it feels just right.

The creamy filling, orange and bright,

Oh, Pumpkin Pie, you're such a sight!

Grab your fork and take a bite,

Warm and cozy, pure delight.

The flavor tickles, soft and mild,

Pumpkin Pie makes every child smile.

A dollop of whipped cream on the top,

A little swirl, oh, don't let it stop!

Creamy and cool, it's the perfect pair,

With Pumpkin Pie, nothing can compare.

It's Time to Eat
Pumpkin Pie

It's more than pie, it's holiday cheer,

A treat we love when autumn is near.

Around the table, we laugh and share,

Pumpkin Pie brings love everywhere.

Each bite tastes like a hug so sweet,

The pumpkin spice just can't be beat.

With every slice, our hearts feel full,

Pumpkin Pie is simply wonderful!

We sing and clap, our voices rise,

"Pumpkin Pie, you're our prize!"

It's a moment of joy, a tasty delight,

Pumpkin Pie makes everything right.

When the last crumb's gone, we'll cheer and say,

"We'll have you again another day!"

Pumpkin Pie, you're a special treat,

It's Time to Eat
Pumpkin Pie

A dessert so perfect, warm, and neat.

So when the leaves fall and the air is cool,

Pumpkin Pie becomes the rule!

With every slice, we're filled with cheer,

Pumpkin Pie time is the best time of year!

And now we know, as the seasons flow,

Pumpkin Pie makes our love grow.

With family near and laughter so bright,

It's Time to Eat
Pumpkin Pie

Pumpkin Pie fills hearts with delight!

ABOUT THE CREATOR

Walter the Educator is one of the pseudonyms for Walter Anderson. Formally educated in Chemistry, Business, and Education, he is an educator, an author, a diverse entrepreneur, and he is the son of a disabled war veteran. "Walter the Educator" shares his time between educating and creating. He holds interests and owns several creative projects that entertain, enlighten, enhance, and educate, hoping to inspire and motivate you. Follow, find new works, and stay up to date with Walter the Educator™ at WaltertheEducator.com

www.ingramcontent.com/pod-product-compliance
Lightning Source LLC
LaVergne TN
LVHW010411070526
838199LV00064B/5259